GOING ON AN AIRPLANE

by Harold T. Rober

BUMBA BOOKS™

LERNER PUBLICATIONS ◆ MINNEAPOLIS

Note to Educators:

Throughout this book, you'll find critical thinking questions. These can be used to engage young readers in thinking critically about the topic and in using the text and photos to do so.

Lerner Publications Company
A division of Lerner Publishing Group, Inc.
241 First Avenue North
Minneapolis, MN 55401 USA

For reading levels and more information, look up this title at www.lernerbooks.com.

Library of Congress Cataloging-in-Publication Data

Names: Rober, Harold T., author.
Title: Going on an airplane / by Harold T. Rober.
Description: Minneapolis, MN : Lerner Publications, a division of Lerner Publishing Group, Inc., [2017] | Series: Bumba books. Fun firsts | Audience: Age 4–7. | Audience: Grade K to Grade 3. | Includes bibliographical references and index.
Identifiers: LCCN 2016024838 (print) | LCCN 2016030608 (ebook) | ISBN 9781512425543 (lb : alk. paper) | ISBN 9781512429275 (pb : alk. paper) | ISBN 9781512427509 (eb pdf)
Subjects: LCSH: Air travel—Juvenile literature. | Aeronautics, Commercial—Passenger traffic—Juvenile literature.
Classification: LCC HE9787 .R63 2017 (print) | LCC HE9787 (ebook) | DDC 387.7/42—dc23

LC record available at https://lccn.loc.gov/2016024838

Manufactured in the United States of America
1 — VP — 12/31/16

LERNER
SOURCE

Expand learning beyond the printed book. Download free, complementary educational resources for this book from our website, www.lerneresource.com.

Table of Contents

Flying in the Sky

This is the airport.

People come here to

travel on airplanes.

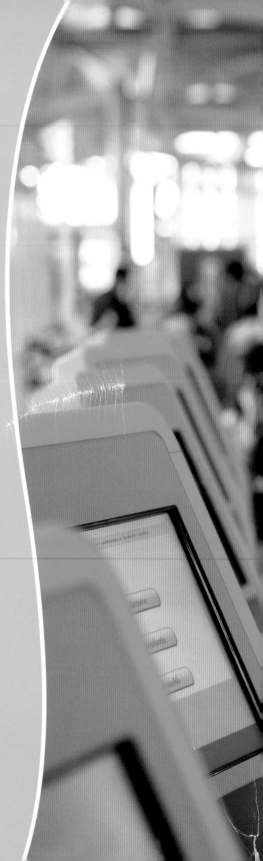

4

People go through a line.

A machine checks

the bags.

This keeps people safe.

Why do you think bags need to be checked at the airport?

People board the airplane.

They find their seats.

They put their bags in special bins.

Why do you think bags have to go in bins?

Next, people fasten their

seat belts.

They learn about the

safety equipment.

Many people read books.

Others watch movies.

Some play video games.

Flight attendants come by.

They bring drinks.

Sometimes they bring snacks.

The airplane lands

in a new city.

Riding in an airplane

is fun!

Flight Supplies

travel bag

snacks

books

blanket

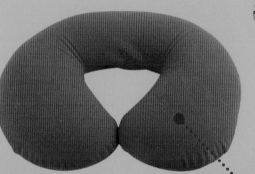
travel pillow

Picture Glossary

board

to get onto an airplane

checks

looks for unsafe things

flight attendants

workers who take care of people on a plane

runway

a strip of land airplanes take off from and land on

23

Index

Read More

Parkes, Elle. *Hooray for Pilots!* Minneapolis: Lerner Publications, 2017.

Rober, Harold T. *Going Camping.* Minneapolis: Lerner Publications, 2017.

Silverman, Buffy. *How Do Jets Work?* Minneapolis: Lerner Publications, 2013.

Photo Credits